A CATHOLIC BIBLE STORYBOOK
FOR YOUNG CHILDREN
With Activities

By Marion Sauer
Illustrated by Theresa Brekan

Book 2

Dedicated to the children of the world in remembrance of Jesus' words: "I tell you that their angels in heaven always behold the face of my Father who is in heaven." Matthew 18:10

A Catholic Bible Storybook Series for Young Children introduces children to God's plan of salvation through well-known Bible stories retold with imaginative detail. Enjoy these colorful renditions that help children imagine Bible times and enter into the scenes. They provide an opportunity for families to explore together the beautiful mystery of God's presence in our lives. They are ideal for reading aloud and sharing family activities that help children understand God's love and purpose for them in everyday life.

God said to Noah, "Make yourself an ark of cypress wood... Go into the ark, you and all your household, for I have seen that you alone are righteous before me in this generation." And Noah did all that the had Lord commanded him. Genesis 6:14, 7:1, 5

A note to parents...

According to Sacred Scripture, the deep waters of the flood encompassed the earth, thoroughly washing away all that was evil. As the waters receded, new life sprang forth. Noah and his family emerged from the ark adorned in the gift of free will to walk as children of God.

They received the promise of God's mercy represented by the light of the rainbow. God gave them instructions that spoke of justice, goodness and righteousness. God's Covenant with Noah covered every living person, family and nation that would spread across the earth. (cf. CCC 71)

The Church points to the Sacrament of Baptism: "The waters of the great flood You made a sign of the waters of Baptism, that makes an end of sin and a new beginning of goodness... God has revealed Himself fully by sending his own Son, in whom he has established his covenant forever" CCC 1219, 73.

God calls children to himself with tenderness and mercy: "Let the little children come to me," Jesus says in Matthew 19:14. We are privileged to help plant seeds of faith in our children, pray for them and watch God's grace work in their lives. We can be joyful instruments of God's love, mercy and goodness to our families, the Church and the world.

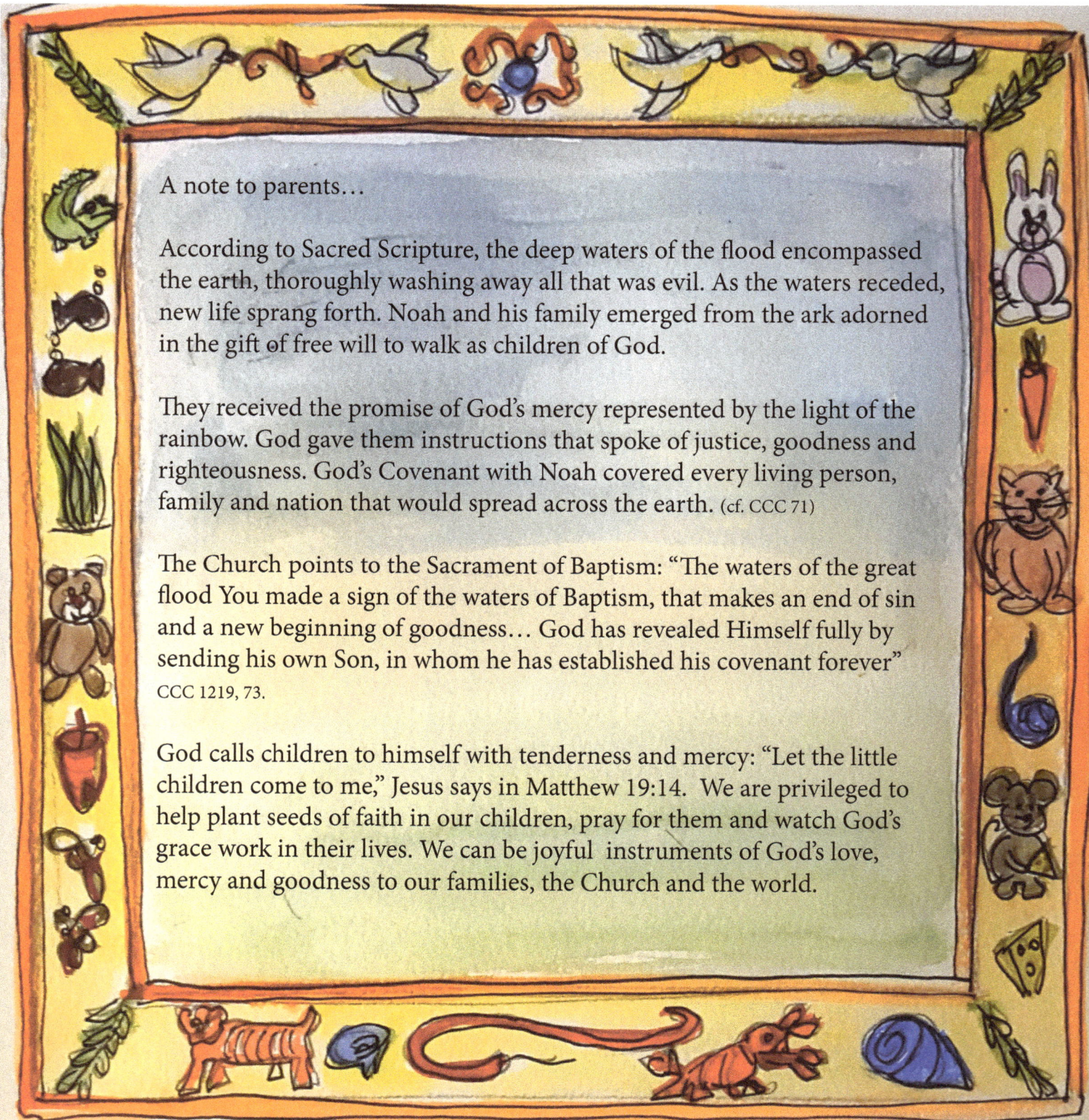

NOAH BUILT
AN ARK FOR GOD

Once long ago, when people were few, Noah had the greatest
adventure he ever knew. He grew up on the family farm.
God prepared him along the way for a special job to do one day.

Imagine young Noah, high in a
tree, waved his arms and cried,
"Look at me!"

Brother laughed and shouted,
"Hurray! You climbed
to the top all the way!"

The sun dipped low.
Noah said, "Time to go!"

They darted past
the olive grove,
splashed through
the creek
and ran straight
into the shed
behind
the garden gate.

"Here I am," Noah said tickling bunny's silky head. He fed her bits of lettuce to eat, and then lay her in the pen to sleep. He poured piglet his favorite oats and gave kitty milk from mama goat.

Picture when Noah was ten, his little fingers pulled the weeds and helped Papa spread the seeds.

He watered herbs, carrots and peas and picked peaches from the trees.

When chores were done, he and Brother played hide-and-seek and chased each other in the swirling creek.

One day Noah learned about his family tree, that faith was part of their legacy.
He heard Papa say,
"Great-grandpa Enoch loved the Lord. God said to him one day,"

'I am the Lord.
I love you.
I made the world for you.

Remember Me
when you see silver stars,
rain, snow
and a bright rainbow.

I speak to you,
my voice in your thoughts.
I speak to your heart
through the love of others.

I am the Lord.
I love you.
Think of Me
and love Me too!'

Perhaps that night Noah lay in bed listening to the crickets sing.
The moon's bright light filled the night and spilled into his room.

Noah raised his eyes to heaven and felt God smile on him.

"I love you, Lord" Noah whispered in the night. Then he
soundly slept 'til morning light.

When Noah turned
fifteen, he and Papa
became a team!

They dug deep lines
in the ground,
guiding old ox to
prepare for the crops.

The red sun went
down to sleep.

Noah said,
"Time to feed old ox,
goats and sheep."

"MOO MOO!"
"BA-A-AH! BA-A-AH!"

They loved their
oats and hay to eat.

The next day Noah worked the vinyards when sunlight laced the hills. Plump grapes gleamed like purple gems, hanging low on curly stems. Noah gathered a basketful of the sweet treat.

To Papa, Mama and Brother's delight, Noah brought some home for dinner that night.

Noah grew up. He met a girl who was nice. She said "Yes!" when he asked, "Will you be my wife?"

Soon children came, Shem, Japheth and Ham.

Noah exclaimed, "Let's honor the Lord and his commands, blessing each other and the land."

"All good gifts come from God's hand."

Noah must have gone to the village one day. He found the people acting in a bad way. They stole his tools and knocked him down. They fought with each other all over the town.

As Noah sadly walked the road back home, he was suddenly caught in a gust of wind.

Noah's great adventure was about to begin!

He heard God's mighty voice call to him.

"My heart is sad," the Lord explained.

"People live in a selfish way. They choose to hurt each other without a care, without any love to share."

"Noah, I am glad you live in the light, making good choices to do what's right."

"A flood is coming to cover the earth, renewing everything to good worth."

"Build an ark, a ship as big as can be. Make it long and wide with a door on its side."

"Bring two animals of every kind with food to keep them alive."

"When the flood comes around, stay in the ark. You'll be safe and sound."

"I will rescue you and your family too!"

Noah replied,
"Whatever you ask, I will do."

Noah ran home and told his wife about God's plan to save their life.

Japeth asked, "Build a great ship?"
Shem chimed in, "Where do we begin?"

Ahh!" Noah said, "We can't miss. With
God's help, together we can do this."

Noah put away the plow and took his boys to the harbor to learn how.

The sailors laughed and shook their heads.
"Ha ha, ho ho! What does farmer Noah know?
A giant ship to hold a zoo? A crazier idea we never knew!"

Noah sadly turned
away. He went to
buy proper tools.

He studied long
hours to learn
all the rules.

Then Noah drew a blueprint with his pen.

Soon Noah and his sons returned to their land.
They climbed trees, cut leaves and stripped branches clean. Trunks
were split into two long planks, sanded smooth and lean.

Boards were fitted, bound and pegged,
to form a huge ship just like God said.

Rub, rub, up and down,
forward, backward, all around.

Pour olive oil to make it shine,
polish the wood smooth and fine.

Splish, splash the bucket swung.

Swish, swash the mop flung -
into the bucket, onto the floor,
water whirling everywhere.

Then pour pine pitch, amber brown,
the best waterproof seal that could be found.

Years passed. Noah and his wife turned gray. The boys grew up and found good wives, adding much joy to their lives.

Work, work year after year. They completed the task with a large cheer.

"Hurray, it's finished!" shouted Shem.
"As tall as clouds," Ham said to them.
"The longest boat that's ever been!" Japheth said with a grin.
"Let's go in!"

The family filled the bottom floor with boxes and baskets of food galore. Up the ramp they rolled barrels of wheat, barley and veggies to eat.

There were packs and stacks of dates and grapes, peas, seeds and chunks of cheese.

Picture bedrooms with blankets made by hand in red, blue and golden sand.

Animal stalls, large and small, were padded with bales of straw. There were nests for birds, boxes for bugs and cages in lines for reptile kinds.

"Our work is almost done," Noah confirmed. "Now let's wait for the animals to come."

One morning Noah heard an incredible sound! Animals galloped over the ground. Insects, reptiles and buzzing bees slithered out of trees. Birdsong echoed in the air as winged creatures flew in from everywhere.

Imagine Noah's serenade
  as he led the great animal parade!

Two elephants swung long grey trunks. Lions roared as they came on
board. Giraffes with long necks followed up next. Burly bears grumbled
and monkeys, like acrobats, twirled and tumbled.

Picture little lambs and brown-eyed calves going up the aisle with
the crocodiles. Black and white skunks scampered fast,
while slim gazelles glided past.

Then came cute kittens, puppies and ponies,
foxes, frogs and spiny hedgehogs.

There were pelicans, penguins and purple peacocks, zebras, lamas and
laughing hyenas. Slimy snails and slippery snakes slid past the spider's
silvery web. Little brown mice ran up and down twice.

At last Noah and his family came on board,
commanded by the word of the Lord.

Whooooo! Shshshshsh!
Craaack! Kaboom!

Lightning streaked across
the sky ripping black
clouds that tumbled by.
Torrents of rain came
in a downpour.

God's mighty hand shut
the door.

Noah saw water rise higher and higher, twirling, swirling, spinning
around like a great ocean covering the ground!

Horses whinnied, bears bellowed, camels

shrieked and mice squeaked.

The family ran from stall to stall trying to calm them all.

They fed the animals day and night, brushed them smooth,
cleaned the stalls, walked the halls and lit the lamps at nightfall.

Noah prayed for God's powerful arm
to protect the ark from all harm.

The ark was tossed and thrown about in a giant hurricane!
Noah counted forty days and forty nights of rain, rain, rain.

On day forty-one the rain finally stopped. Noah saw sunlight glisten on the sparkling sea where the mountains should be!

Noah sent Raven to fly around, but Raven couldn't find any dry ground.

He let out Dove who returned to his hand when she also couldn't find land.

"Fly again, Dove!" Noah said after a while.

Wind blew swiftly over the ground.
The water slowly sank down, down, down.

This time, Noah was happy to see,
Dove brought back a leaf from an olive tree.

Then Dove flew away and didn't come back. Noah's ark landed
on the mountains of Ararat.

Wet ground finally dried. Noah flung open the doors wide. "What a hullabaloo!" he cried.

Animals, birds and creeping things tumbled and slid, fluttered and flew, streaming out of the ark. Each sought a new home to make a fresh start.

Noah built an altar to God while gathering his family.
"Thank you, Lord, for rescuing us," they prayed joyfully.

Out of the clouds they heard God's word.

"I promise you and your descendants too;
and all living creatures within-
A FLOOD WILL NEVER COVER THE WHOLE EARTH AGAIN!"

"The rainbow is a sign of my covenant promise
for all the world to see."

"Now have many children, fill the earth
and treat each other with dignity."

"My love will light your way.
Be good to each other every day."

Imagine their songs and candles lit,
"This is the day the Lord has made.
Let us rejoice and be glad in it!"

God blessed the descendants of Noah as they spread across the world.
They were people of many colors and cultures,
all made in God's image and love.

Family Activities

LOOK AND SEE

5
olive trees

6
grapevines

2
wagons with hay

3
donkeys

4
doves with olive branches

4
monkeys in trees

2

colorful peacocks

5

mountains

10

shiny raindrops

3

rainbows

1

Noah's ark

6

slimy snails

I AM A CHILD OF GOD

Scripture verse: 1 John 3:1
"See what love the Father has given us, that we should be called children of God; and so we are."

Ideas to share:
Jesus tells us in the Bible that God is our heavenly Father. I am a child of God. I am part of God's family. At my baptism I received God's life of grace. God has special plans for my life.

Activity: Picture Sharing Time
Make a special time with your family to look at pictures of your Baptism, the baptismal candle and any other articles saved. Invite your godparents and family members to share their memories of your baptismal day. If you haven't received the Sacrament of Baptism yet, look at baby pictures when you were born. Talk about God's love in creating you.

Let's pray:
Dear Father in heaven, I am happy to be a child of God. I love you and give my heart to You! Help me to love more like you. Amen.

GOD IS ALWAYS WITH ME

Scripture verse: Psalm 23:4
"I fear no evil; for you are with me."

Ideas to share:
When I am afraid, I remember that God is always with me. If I am hurt, lonely or sad, I think of God and pray. He lifts my heart, and I feel safe again. The Bible tells us that God knows and understands our feelings. He is everywhere watching over me.

Activity: Feeling Faces
Divide card stock into four squares. With a sharpie draw a face in each square expressing a different feeling: happy, silly, sad, mad. Use watercolors to show what you think the emotion looks like.

Let's pray:
Thank you, Lord, for always being there with me no matter how I am feeling. I know your love is always with me wherever I go. Help me to love you more each and every day. Amen.

MY GUARDIAN ANGEL

Scripture verse: Psalm 23:4
Psalm 91:11 "For he will command his angels concerning you to guard you in all your ways."

Ideas to share:
The rainbow in Noah's story reminds us that God is taking care of us. The Bible tells that God gives me a guardian angel to protect me. My guardian angel helps me to live as a child of God. We might not see them, but guardian angels are our faithful friends, always with us. I can praise God and thank Him for giving me my guardian angel.

Activity: Angel Message
Talk about how your guardian angel can help you each day. Think about what your guardian angel might look like. Draw a picture of you with your guardian angel near you. Write a special message. Use your favorite colors. With another family member recite the prayer to the guardian angels (below).

Let's pray:
Angel of God, my guardian dear, through whom God's love protects me here. Ever this day be at my side to light and guard, to rule and guide. Amen.

GOD'S GOOD GIFTS

Scripture verse: James 1:17
"Every good thing and every perfect gift is from above, coming down from the Father of lights."

Ideas to share:
God loves us as a good father loves his children. He gives gifts because he loves us. He gives the beauty of the earth, the love of family, fun with friends, and many special things. The most special gift of all is the Lord's never-ending love.

Activity: Family Gratitude Jar
Decorate a jar and put it on your dinner table. During the week at dinner, jot down on small slips of paper what you are grateful to God for. Place the notes inside the jar. On Sunday or other family time, read the notes aloud. Finish with the prayer of thanks.

Let's pray:
Thank you, Lord, for your wonderful gifts, especially for your love. Help me to be kind and share your gifts with others. Amen.

www.ingramcontent.com/pod-product-compliance
Lightning Source LLC
Chambersburg PA
CBHW040303100426
42811CB00011B/1350